Isle of Wight Smugglers' Pubs

Terry Townsend

To my wife Carol
for in every sense this is her book, too

ACKNOWLEDGEMENTS

Thanks also to Adrienne Bradney-Smith
and Brenda and Tony Stables
for their continued help and support

Terry Townsend's other Halsgrove titles include:
Once upon a Pint – A Readers' Guide to the Literary Pubs & Inns of Dorset & Somerset,
Kent Smugglers' Pubs, Dorset Smugglers' Pubs, Jane Austen's Hampshire,
Jane Austen & Bath, Jane Austen's Kent, Hampshire Smugglers' Pubs

First published in Great Britain in 2016

Copyright © Terry Townsend 2016

British Library Cataloguing-in-Publication Data
A CIP record for this title is available from the
British Library

ISBN 978 0 85710 103 7

PiXZ Books
Halsgrove House, Ryelands Business Park,
Bagley Road, Wellington, Somerset TA21 9PZ
Tel: 01823 653777
Fax: 01823 216796
email: sales@halsgrove.com

An imprint of Halstar Ltd, part of the
Halsgrove group of companies
Information on all Halsgrove titles is
available at: www.halsgrove.com

Printed and bound in China by
Everbest Printing Investment Ltd

CONTENTS

Introduction

'The Isle of Wight is England in miniature. Somewhere on the Island you will find an example of the mainland's landscape. There are over 60 miles of varied coastline – high cliffs, sheltered coves, marshes and seaside towns with sandy beaches. Inland there are high downs, woodlands, picturesque villages, river valleys and miles of open farmland.'

Isle of Wight – The Complete Guide. *Roy Brinton 2006.*

Free Trading

From around 1700 Britain was waging war in some part of the world well-nigh continuously against the forces of France, Holland, Spain and eventually with the American colonists. By the mid eighteenth century foreign war had become an accepted way of life in these islands.

To fund the conflicts successive governments imposed taxes on the importation of a wide range of luxury goods and in so doing the law makers unwittingly created a climate in the country for the establishment of serious organised crime.

However, the black cloud came with the opportunity of a silver lining. Buying tax-free goods abroad and selling to an eager home market was a very profitable, if somewhat dangerous pastime. This 'Free Trading' as it became known to those involved, was an inevitable result of punitive taxation.

George Morland's 1792 painting shows men unloading tubs they have collected from a vessel lying off shore.

This picture of smugglers' cottages at
Calbourne supports Roy Brinton's assertion that:
'The Isle of Wight is England in miniature'.

Smuggling grew to enormous proportions, becoming an important element of the country's economy, particularly along the south coast of England. Many consignments of contraband were despatched to the great houses in the Island like Nunwell, Arreton Manor, Appuldurcombe and Carisbrooke Castle as well as pubs and inns, scattered farms and cottages.

A Profitable Partnership

Until about 150 years ago, the mainland population regarded the Isle of Wight almost as a foreign country. They looked upon its inhabitants with suspicion and some hostility – sentiments which were of course reciprocated. Island folk scathingly nicknamed mainlanders as 'Overners'.

However, there was an aspect of life which Islanders and Overners generally agreed on and that was tax evasion, in the form of smuggling in which they became willing partners.

The Island's gentry, like the family from Nunwell House, were good customers of local smugglers.

Many stone cottages and farm buildings across the Island display an etching of a galleon believed to be a smugglers' mark.

Below: Bottle ends built into brickwork indicate a safe house for smugglers.

Taxes have always been unpopular with most of society but in Georgian England were widely resented by a rural population on the poverty line.

The Isle of Wight's prominent smuggling role can largely be attributed to its offshore location with its sheltered coves and sandy beaches. Much of the contraband shipped by Island smugglers was destined for mainland customers.

For eighteenth and early nineteenth-century smugglers the Island became a natural forward base for traffic to and from the continent. Separated from the mainland by The Solent, this diamond-shaped landmass was a natural gift to the free traders and developed into a main dumping depot where contraband could be stockpiled reasonably safely.

Wight smugglers took full advantage of the geography, using their homeland base as a giant stepping stone and unique staging post for contraband purchased in Northern France and the Channel Islands.

Back of Wight

Most of the people involved were those from 'Back of Wight' and the community of 'The Undercliff'. Back of Wight

Built in 1704, Moortown Cottage in Moortown Lane, Brighstone appears to have been designed for the express purpose of concealing contraband. The present owners Alan and Denise Kaill offer a quintessential English B&B.

is land on the southern side of the downs in the west with the boundary following the curve of the downs till they meet the sea near St Catherine's Point. It is an area very cut off from the rest of the Island, comprising small villages strung out along or near the coast from the southern central tip of St Catherine's, through Chale, Shorewell, Brighstone, Mottistone, Hulverstone and Brook ending at Freshwater on the western edge.

The main part of Back of Wight is formed of a large bay 18 miles long. The shore is edged by cliffs averaging 300 feet high from Freshwater to Compton, broken at two points, Grange Chine and Brook Chine, which provide the only easy, natural access to the sea through steep gorges. Stretching out from this coast are three ledges of resistant rock, the Brook, Brighstone and Atherfield ledges, on which many ships have been wrecked over the years.

In the eighteenth century there was a succession of stormy winters increasing the number of wrecks on Back of Wight's

The main part of Back of Wight is formed
of a large bay 18 miles long. The shore
is edged by cliffs averaging around
300 feet high from Freshwater to Compton.

coast. Salvage and theft were combined with thriving local smuggling. Many local buildings were constructed in part from timber plundered from wrecks. James Wheeler, a local man, kept a record between 1746 and 1808 during which 60 ships came to grief in Chale Bay alone. It was not until the wreck of the *Clarendon* in 1836 that something was done to diminish this.

The Undercliff

Smugglers' caves in the cliffs at Freshwater Bay.

The Undercliff is the continuation of the southern coastline stretching from Blackgang around St Catherine's Point to Bonchurch just beyond Ventnor. It is cut off from the main plateau by inland cliffs rising in places to two hundred feet, climbable only here and there in the major 'faults'. This curiously isolated stretch of land was regarded justifiably with

The opportunist landlord of the White Lion at Niton used to row out to homeward-bound ships to purchase tea, silks, gloves, tobacco and similar luxuries at duty-free prices.

fear by the Islanders for it contained as lawless a community as any in the country.

Smugglers from Niton, Whitwell and St Lawrence were particularly active along the Undercliff but due to landslips and erosion the cliffs and coastline have undergone dramatic changes since the days of the free traders.

One of the smuggling leaders at St Lawrence was 'Captain' Harvey, who lived at 'The Duck', a wayside unlicensed house known as a 'shebeen' or 'pop-shop', where ne'er-do-wells of the district congregated and where a continuous trade in many kinds of smuggled goods was carried on. Prim and respectable, with no hint of its colourful past, the Duck still exists, and is now called Spring Cottage.

Illicit goods, landed on these southern shores, were transported north across the Island, then shipped beyond Spithead and The Solent to the coasts of Hampshire and Dorset.

The Profit Motive

The illegal trade grew at a prodigious rate fuelled by the resulting profits. In 1724 tea could be bought from continental suppliers at 6d or a shilling a pound, then sold in England for six or seven times this amount. Contemporary estimates say 80% of all tea drunk in England had no duty paid on it.

By 1760 800 products were liable for duty but by 1810 the number had grown to 2100 items. Besides tea the Island's smugglers' favourite goods were brandy, gin, tobacco, lace, and silk, all subject to the highest taxes. Casks of brandy or gin were the stock-in-trade of most smuggling voyages. Gin (or Geneva) could be produced for as little as 2 shillings a gallon in continental distilleries and

sold in the UK for four times that price. French brandy acquired at 5 shillings a gallon could be sold to wealthy Islanders or mainland dealers for five times that amount.

A Revenue Cutter in pursuit of a smugglers' lugger crossing The Solent.

Although Britain was at war with France, French authorities actively encouraged the smuggling trade. The population in general did not consider smuggling a crime. Merchandise paid for in France belonged to the purchaser and a crime occurred only when attempts were made to import customs listed goods without payment of duty.

On the Island most poor fishing families supplemented their meagre income with a little smuggling.

Smuggling here flourished for a hundred years or more with an ease and expertise unsurpassed along the English Channel. Contraband traffic reached its peak between 1780 and 1840, when it is said four of every five Undercliff residents played some part in it.

Renowned smuggler 'Pound-hammer' Kingswell from Luccombe.

A Family Affair

On the mainland organised smuggling often involved large gangs or 'companies' of smugglers including financiers, book-keepers and extensive transport teams with their bodyguards. Others were employed as lookouts with special lamps and lights to guide the landers and to warn of impending danger.

Because of the Island's much smaller size, the enterprise here was more of a family affair, smugglers who bought and landed the goods were often involved with transport and distribution. The exploits of some Island families including the Kingswells of Luccombe, the Wheelers of Blackgang and the smuggling Conway brothers of Totland have become legendary.

The economics of each smuggling foray followed a standard pattern based on co-operative principles. Each village had a trusted leader selected for his skill, energy, judgment and presence of mind who carried out all the preliminary organisation as well as leading the actual 'run'. Each shareholder subscribed a sum to cover a share of the expenses together with whatever investment they required in spirits, tea, tobacco, silks etc.

Most money was made on spirits, usually obtained in 4½ gallon casks at a price of fourteen shillings on the French coast. The expense of the outgoing run was standard at three shillings a cask and a further three shillings per cask was charged for the homeward run and subsequent landing of the cargo. Thus, 4½ gallons of proof spirits would cost one pound on delivery to its appointed cellar in the Island.

The spirits would then be diluted with an equal quantity of water, burnt sugar being added as colouring. The original investment of twenty shillings would now be worth fifty shillings, but probably a large amount would readily be sold at half-a-crown a bottle returning an even larger profit.

Thomas Rowlandson's cartoon of a female smuggler revealing contraband hidden under her clothing.

The Female Smugglers

Thomas Rowlandson's cartoon 'Rigging the Smuggler' looks at first sight to be far-fetched until compared with the list of Customs Prosecutions in the Island between 1830 and 1851 when twenty-seven women were prosecuted for smuggling (see page 57).

Smugglers' vessels

Two kinds of boats were used for smuggling. Most in demand along the Undercliff coast were lightly built,

broad beamed, four or six oared rowing boats, which, in reasonable weather could make the crossing to France in a few hours.

The crew of a lightly-built, broad-beamed rowing boat, ferrying contraband from a large sailing vessel anchored offshore.

Rowing boats could manage a return journey with as many as 40 x 4½ gallon casks. The outward trip was usually accomplished without incident but, on the return, known as 'running the cargo', a very strict watch had to be maintained for Coastguard Cutters which might be on the lookout, having probably been warned of the boat's absence on shore.

The second type were the sailing vessels of 10 to 40 tons, which had stowage for 100 to 250 casks, and normally hailed from Bembridge or St Helens.

Avoiding discovery

Precautions against discovery while 'running the cargo' were many and varied. Perhaps the most effective was the 'outboard warp' consisting of a rope lashed around the gunwales. Casks were fastened to it by their individual slings while cork floats, to act as buoys, and stone sinkers were also attached to the warp at intervals.

Weights such as these were attached to kegs to sink them below the surface for later retrieval.

In an emergency the whole cargo could be sunk out of sight by giving the warp one smart blow with a machete. The next day the cargo could be gathered, along with the crab pots from another row of cork floats bobbing nearby.

The usual 'beat' of the Coastguards was well plotted before-hand and the times at which they passed the appointed landing place noted. 'When the coast was clear', the landing party shone a light directed towards the incoming vessel. The craft then approached as close as possible to the beach and the casks untied and dragged ashore.

The tub carriers then took over, lashing the casks together in pairs, using the 18-inch thongs of the sling harness round each one. Every man would shoulder a pair of kegs. If the landing party was able to use horses, each animal would be loaded with six tubs and, in a matter of five minutes, the whole cargo would be on its way into hiding.

Grappling hooks were used to drag the sea bed for kegs.

At this stage the danger was by no means past. It might be a matter of seconds to cut a warp and sink a cargo out of sight at sea but it was entirely another matter to dispose of two casks if you came face to face with a Preventive Man, or to hide a horse with its load of contraband in the darkness of a country lane.

In spite of some gallant honest men among them, most Customs Riding Officers were ineffectual or corrupt.

The Customs Men

Throughout the eighteenth century, when most of the King's men were engaged in overseas wars, smugglers had it very much their own way. There was little difficulty and comparatively little danger, because the Preventive Service was weak and inefficient.

It was difficult to recruit men, the pay being grossly inadequate and the work exacting and tedious. Those who did join, in the early days, were usually drawn from ill-educated classes and were known, on occasion, to covertly acquiesce and sometimes even to share, in the profits obtained from smuggling ventures.

Most smuggled cargo escaped detection as Revenue Men were often inept, 'in liquor', or corrupt. Large rewards offered for information were rarely claimed despite whole adult populations of towns and villages having full knowledge or involvement in the trade.

The main threat to the Lander and his team came from the 'Customs Riding Officers' who were expected to be out in all weathers patrolling at least 4 miles of coastline and keeping watch up to 10 miles inland for signs of smuggling activity. This unenviable lonely task was made worse by the active resentment of much of the local population.

Many Riding Officers died as a result of violence or under suspicious circumstances. It is said that on one occasion Preventive Officers who called at the Highdown Inn at Totland seeking evidence of contraband were never seen to leave and no one ever heard of them again. It is alleged that after being knocked unconscious they were taken to the top of the Down and their bodies thrown on to the rocks hundreds of feet below.

William Arnold

William Arnold, father of Dr Thomas Arnold the renowned headmaster of Rugby School, became the Collector of Excise for the Island in 1777. In later years Thomas Arnold often spoke of his happy childhood at Cowes, where his lifelong interest in ships, and flags of all nations, and his early enthusiasm for history and geography, were inspired by his father.

William Arnold, zealous Collector of Customs, became the scourge of Isle of Wight smugglers.

William, who was most zealous for the authority of the Crown, knew what he was facing because his own father was a Supervisor of Excise for Poole in Dorset. When William first took up his duties, free traders would flaunt the Customs openly and often landed their cargoes during daylight, under the very eyes of the Customs Men, who could do little to stop them.

Fairly soon after being appointed to Cowes, William Arnold reported to the Board of Customs that: 'within the last three years smuggling has increased upon this coast to an alarming degree.' He was particularly concerned about armed luggers: 'which are so large no revenue cruiser can keep pace with them.'

Living at Cowes for twenty-four years, William had many and varied duties. In addition to seizing smuggling vessels, he was responsible for the registration of new vessels and for giving clearance to local ships, as well as all seagoing merchant vessels in the area. He had a marked talent in dealing with people, and was a tolerant and understanding man as well as a champion of his men's rights.

The measures he took at sea, including fitting out a large armed vessel, the *Swan,* at his own expense eventually turned the tide against smugglers.

Control of inland smuggling was also under Arnold's juris-diction. His Riding Officers patrolled between Cowes and Newtown Harbour and skirted the whole coast via the Needles, Atherfield, Niton, Shanklin and beyond Culver

Downs to Brading Harbour; thence from Ryde to East Cowes to complete the circuit.

After his death the Customs Men regressed in their efforts, and in 1832 it was recorded that nearly all Islanders were 'more or less concerned with smuggling'. Another survey in 1836 estimated 80% of the population was consuming contraband spirits, tobacco and tea.

Punishments

Any offenders unable to disguise their ability as experienced seamen (and most of them had been since their youth) were dragged off to spend five years on board a man-of-war. This was of course continuous service without leave, although there would be remission for good behaviour. James Bucket of Brighstone was convicted at Winchester Court for smuggling in 1832, sentenced to five years service and was released with four month's remission for good conduct.

If violence was used and a Coastguard was injured, a far more severe penalty was imposed including transportation. A £100 fine was the usual consequence of being caught 'concealing and conveying' smuggled goods. For those who could not pay, six months in Winchester Gaol followed, with or without hard labour, usually depending on the amount of resistance involved during apprehension.

When Chief Coastguard Officer of Ryde, William Thomas Ricard V.C. heard he had been awarded the Victoria Cross and the Legion of Honour for bravery during the Crimean War, he imbibed too freely and lost his previously earned Good Conduct Medal.

For most labourers the fine of £100 would be equivalent of more than two years' wages, and unless paid by the smuggling organiser would automatically result in imprisonment with the felon's family forced to rely on the parish for sustenance.

The Island finally acquired its own prison in 1863 when Parkhurst military hospital building was converted for the purpose. From its beginnings, as a prison for young male offenders, Parkhurst was subject to fierce criticism by the public, politicians and the press for its harsh regime initially including the use of leg irons.

It became a particular focus of criticism for reformers campaigning against the use of imprisonment of children, most notably by Mary Carpenter. The Parkhurst Boys were transported to Australia and New Zealand during the decade from 1842. 1500 boys between the ages of twelve and eighteen were transported, and apprenticed to disguise their status as convicts.

Plundering wrecks prompted a fine between £5 to £20 and a prison sentence from one month to six months hard labour. In 1837, twelve-year-old Harry Lane of School Green, Freshwater was fined £100 mitigated to £50 and sent to gaol 'until the Penalty shall be paid'. Caroline Tizzard was arrested in 1837 when she was only nine. Unable to pay the £5 fine she was committed to the 'Common Gaol' or town lockup at Newport.

A publican and a butcher from St Helens were each fined £200 for attempting to bribe a Preventive Man. Figures available for the period between 1830 and 1851 show there were well over 200 convictions for smuggling on the Island, with eight of the guilty being Frenchmen.

Wrecking

'One of the most notorious eighteenth-century crimes receiving the sanction of the entire local community' is how Tobias Smollett described 'wrecking' in his *New History of England* published during 1757/8. However, the word 'plundering' should be substituted for 'wrecking'.

Legends, perpetuated by novelists like Daphne Du Maurier in *Jamaica Inn*, lead some to believe that ships were deliberately lured into danger by a display of false lights and wreck survivors callously murdered eliminating possible witnesses to the heinous crime.

The truth is, tricks like this would simply not work. Mariners interpret a light as indicating land, and so avoid them if they cannot identify them. Moreover, oil lanterns cannot be seen at any distance over water at night, unless they are large, fitted with mirrors or lenses, and mounted at a great height (i.e. in a lighthouse). No surviving captain of a wrecked ship ever charged that he had been led astray by a false light. This is really a slur on seafaring smuggling communities. With the greatest respect for the sea and sympathy for those who found themselves in peril, smugglers had to be expert seamen. Early Island lifeboat crews would have been smugglers to a man.

There is not a single recorded instance of deliberate wrecking and the inhumane murder of survivors but plundering is an entirely different matter. Wrecked vessels along the south coast of the Island were considered to be 'God given' and the goods and materials they provided viewed as precious and necessary bounty to alleviate the harsh and meagre existence of coast dwellers.

Whilst certainly not provoking wrecks by the use of false lights, Islanders nevertheless viewed stormy weather with a certain anticipatory pleasure. William Meade Falkner the author of *Moonfleet*, maintained that children of coast dwellers were taught an old rhyme: 'Blow wind, rise storm, Ship ashore before morn!' Fishermen talked about 'a good wreck season' just as they would about fishing prospects and then 'thank Providence for it' but these were the same men who rushed to launch the lifeboat when there was a prospect of saving a life.

In 1859 the first lifeboats were installed at Brighstone and Brook; they conducted many famous rescues and are commemorated in Brighstone Museum, which has many artefacts of the era. Today's definition of wrecking is the practice of taking valuables from a shipwreck which has foundered close to shore. Often an unregulated activity of opportunity in coastal communities, wrecking has been subjected to increasing regulation and evolved into what is now known as marine salvage.

Coastguards

Smuggling had been at its height during the mid to late eighteenth century. It was then that the Ryde organiser of smuggling David Boyce accumulated sufficient capital to build Appley House with extensive cellars to store contraband.

The tide really began to turn against the free traders after the 1815 Battle of Waterloo, when the attention of the armed services could be directed to combating domestic smuggling. In 1817 the Royal Navy began using blockade techniques and the 'Preventative Water Guard', the forerunner of the Coast Guard, was founded. Their main purpose was to guard the coast to stop the landing of prohibited goods and to search inshore waters for goods previously sunk close to the shore.

Eventually Coastguard stations were positioned at 3-mile intervals all along the coast so officers could keep in touch by semaphore. As the Coastguard's grip tightened at Back of Wight, stations were established at Atherfield (1825), Freshwater (1827) and Brook (1829). Most of the men came from Cornwall and were resented by the local population. Two Brook Coastguards beaten up at Freshwater Gate in 1835 were confined to bed for five weeks afterwards.

After 1831 when the old-fashioned 'runs' became impossible, patrolling Coastguards were constantly out in their boats 'creeping' with grapnels to locate sunken tubs.

After 1856, when the Admiralty took over control of the Coastguards, a policy of building terraces of cottages for the men and their families was adopted. These houses, which are still a familiar sight on the Island, are in spectacular beachside positions where no planning permission to build would possibly be granted today. Sometimes it must have been quite

The Old Gaol House in Winchester is now a Wetherspoon Pub.

a crush in these small cottages with many families extending to more than a dozen children.

By this time the Coastguard Service improved so greatly that contraband running was becoming a highly dangerous profession and a reduction in excise duties was ruining the profits. This initiative, together with a gradual relaxation in taxation on the smugglers' favoured goods, saw the decline and eventual demise of the 'Golden Age' of smuggling.

The Smugglers' Pub

The nerve centre of smuggling operations was predominantly the local pub, where plots were hatched, arrangements for transportation agreed and runs commissioned. The smugglers' pub served as a meeting place, recruitment centre, secret storage facility, distribution depot and valued customer.

Wrecked vessels provided goods and materials which were considered to be 'God given' and viewed as precious and necessary bounty to alleviate a harsh and meagre existence.

The pub proprietors were often directly involved in smuggling. The opportunist landlord of the White Lion at Niton used to row out to homeward bound ships to purchase tea, silks, gloves, tobacco and similar luxuries at duty-free prices.

This is a guide to a significant number of authentic pubs patronised over two centuries ago by Isle of Wight smugglers. These wonderful old buildings with their low-beamed ceilings, flagstone floors, inglenook fireplaces and secret hiding places are where, with a little imagination, one can sense the desperate days of the free traders.

In 1859 the first lifeboats were installed at Brighstone and Brook; they took part in many famous rescues and are commemorated in Brighstone Museum.

REAL PUB FOOD

TRADITIONAL
BEERS & ALES

SKY SPORTS TV

LARGE GARDEN

A WARM
WELCOME

Family
Inn

SERVING FOOD
ALL DAY

BOUNCY
CASTLE

GARDEN

Turn right and 30 yards here

THE PUBS

Shalfleet
New Inn
Main Road, Shalfleet, PO30 4NS
Tel: 01983 531314
www.thenew-inn.co.uk

One of the main smuggling routes from the south (or Back of Wight) up to the north coast, passed through Shalfleet parish. At this tapering westerly side of the Island only 6 miles separates the Undercliff at Brook from Newton Bay on The Solent. Today this ancient smugglers' trail is dissected by the busy A3054 Yarmouth to Newport road cutting through the small village of Shalfleet, 3 miles east of Yarmouth.

The characterful New Inn dates from 1743.

Tables and benches outside the pub face the quiet Mill Lane.

The New Inn on the main road faces Mill Lane at a T junction and from here it is an easy twenty minute stroll to the quaint old boat yard, all the way affording wonderful views of the estuary and its bird life.

The quiet country road becomes Shalfleet Quay Lane, before ending at a small quay on the estuary of the Newtown River complex where waters meet and flow through marshy mud flats into Newtown Bay.

The Shalfleet parish and Newbridge in particular (a mile south of Shalfleet) had a bad reputation in the early nineteenth century for lawlessness, drunkenness and smuggling. Gangs of free traders worked this area very effectively, sometimes combining with the Compton, Brook and Brighstone gangs to conceal and distribute contraband. Island smugglers also operated from the shores of Hamstead; a wild and sparsely populated area, one and a half miles northwest of Shalfleet.

Goddards Fuggle-Dee-Dum, Ringwood Best and Sharp's Doom Bar are on hand pump.

This quintessential English country pub has inglenook fireplaces, flagstone floors and original beamed ceilings.

Pine tables, settles and country-style chairs add to the cottagey feel of the interior.
Below: The rambling rooms have plenty of charm, with warming fires and walls decorated with yachting and fishing artefacts.

Newtown, a mile northwest of the pub, was also a hotbed of smugglers. Once a busy port and one of the Island's most important towns, it was devastated by fire after a French raid of 1377 which also saw an attack on Newport from which it never fully recovered.

To the rear, on a raised level, is a dining room extension with plain walls above match-boarding.

Newtown Creek was once a deep harbour which could take ships up to 500 tons but all that remains of the town today are a few cottages, a church, town hall and the former smugglers' pub. Fortunately the properties and much of the surrounding land is now in the ownership of the National Trust thus ensuring the preservation of this unique area.

Dating from 1743, the New Inn, oozes character with inglenook fireplaces, flagstone floors and authentic beamed ceilings. The original cottage section of the pub appears to be

Shalfleet Quay, with its wonderful estuary views, is an approximate forty minute walk from the New Inn.

The old Town Hall at Newtown dates from 1700 and is one of the handful of remaining buildings. It is open to the public and houses an exhibition of the Borough's history.

little changed from the days when fishermen sat on the settles swapping tales of the sea and smuggling.

To the rear, on a raised level, is a dining room extension with plain walls above match-boarding decorated in pastel pink. The scrubbed pine tables and country-style chairs contribute to the cottagey feel and there is an excellent collection of photographs of the pub in bygone days. Outside, behind the tiny car parking bay, a raised decking area with picnic sets provides a view over the surrounding countryside.

Goddards Fuggle-Dee-Dum, Ringwood Best and Sharp's Doom Bar are on hand pump plus farm cider and 11 wines by the glass. There may be double sittings at busy times in summer and dogs are allowed only in areas with stone floors.

The former pub at Newtown, once the haunt of smugglers, has been a private dwelling since 1916. Note the sea-facing small window on the gable end, perfect for signalling with a light.

Wootton Bridge
The Sloop Inn

Mill Square, Wootton, PO33 4HS

Tel: 01983 882544

www.crowncarveries.co.uk

Since the time of the free traders the Sloop Inn has increased in size about six fold, annexing the next door cottage and extending at the rear towards the creek.

Wootton Bridge is situated midway between the towns of Ryde and Newport, which are 7 miles apart on the north-west coast of the Island. Originally a separate village at the crossing-point of Wootton Creek it is now merged with the village of Wootton centered on the old parish church of St Edmund, and the hamlet of Wootton Common to the south. Today this combined settlement is often referred to simply as 'Wootton'.

There is a pleasant outside area at the water's edge with some covered seating and a large beer garden.

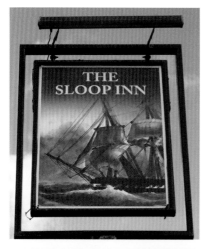

After the Napoleonic Wars, and until late in the nine-teenth-century The Sloop Inn at Wootton was a smugglers port of call.

During the smuggling era local fishermen traded very profitably with the French, buying brandy at one shilling a gallon. Evading the two Preventive Men stationed at Fishbourne, smugglers transported their contraband inland up Wootton Creek. Many an illicit cargo was hidden in St Edmund's churchyard with the connivance of the clergy.

The highly successful marketing strategy here focuses on a three meat carvery on offer every day at an incredibly low price.

There is no record of a Wootton smuggler having been caught, but Thomas Sivell was pursued by a Preventive Cutter, and shot dead. His grave may still be seen in nearby Binstead cemetery, where the inscription reads:

To the memory of THOs SIVELL who was
cruelly shot on board his sloop by some officers of
customs of the Port of Portsmouth on the 15th
June 1785 at the age of 64 years leaving a
disconsolate widow & family.
All you that pass pray look and see
How soon my life was took from me
By those officers as you hear
They spilled my Blood that was so dear
But God is Good and just and true
And will reward each to their due

The grave of Wootton smuggler Thomas Sivell can be seen in nearby Binstead cemetery.

Mr James Henry Young of Fishbourne, who was born in 1839 and died at the age of ninety-seven, left a record of the far off days when he assisted local fishermen in picking up brandy kegs which had been weighted and deposited overboard. The clandestine operation naturally took place at night and smugglers would wait for an all clear signal flashed from the back door of the Sloop Inn. They then glided their craft to the entrance of a tunnel running under the inn and connected with an adjacent house called Ivy Hall. Here waiting men would hurriedly hide the cargo under the stairs. Some years ago a previous owner of Ivy Hall called in the fire brigade to survey the tunnel and it was recommended that it be sealed due to the risk of methane gas. The present owners of this lovely house offer an exceptionally good B&B.

At least three hundred years old, the Sloop Inn was originally the miller's house for Wootton Tide Mill which was

An information panel near the pub details aspects of Wootton Bridge's history.

Smugglers would wait for an all clear signal flashed from the back door of the Sloop Inn before gliding their craft up the creek to the entrance of a tunnel which ran under the pub.

In this early illustration a 'cock horse' and pair are seen pulling a heavily-laden coach over the causeway and timber bridge.

demolished in 1963. It also served as the ferry house, long before the first bridge was built. Later, after the Napoleonic Wars, and until late in the nineteenth century it was a smugglers port of call.

Since the time of the free traders the pub has increased in size about six fold, annexing the adjacent cottage and extending at the rear towards the creek. The highly successful marketing strategy here focuses on a three meat carvery on offer every day at an incredibly low price.

A pleasant outside area at the water's edge has some covered seating and a large beer garden. Although the Sloop is predominately a family pub it does seem to appeal to a huge range of customers both young and old, attracted by the lovely setting and value for money dining. Beers include Marstons's EPA and Ringwood Best.

Ivy House, which was connected to the Sloop Inn by a smugglers' tunnel.

The stone-built house left of the Vine Inn was 'The Sailor's Home' pub during the smuggling era.

St Helens
The Vine Inn
Upper Green Road, St Helens PO33 1UJ

Tel: 01983 872337

www.thevinesthelens.co.uk

St Helens sits at the mouth of Brading Haven in the rural northeast of the Island. The village straddles the crest of an undulating hill some 50m above sea level and overlooks Brading Marshes and The Duver, a coastal plain one mile to its west. Here the village green is said to be the largest in England. Surrounded by houses, stone built cottages, shops and a pub, the Green provides a lovely setting for the hub of village life. Our interest is in three of the properties: a cottage named 'Freefolk', the Vine Inn and the small stone house standing immediately next to the Vine.

One of the most famous smugglers of St Helens was hard drinking fisherman Richard 'Dickie' Dawes. Many stories are

still told of his encounters with the Preventive Men. Sandbanks close to Bembridge Harbour present a hazard to shipping. To import his contraband cargo of brandy, silk and tobacco Dickie often ran the gauntlet of Customs Men through a narrow channel in the banks still known as 'Dickie Dawes Gut'.

The booty once landed would often be hidden beneath tombstones in the churchyard of St Helens Old Church before being brought inland along secret passages leading to the Priory and village.

On the edge of the huge green, the Vine Inn is the perfect place from which to enjoy village cricket.

This happy couple enjoying a quiet drink help train guide dogs for the blind.

Dickie, and his wife Jane lived in Freefolk Cottage in Upper Green Road, a dozen houses east of the Vine. They had ten children, only four of whom lived to adulthood. One, a daughter named Sophie, was to become scandalously famous.

As a child Sophie was employed in picking winkles off St Helens beach but her father's intemperate habits forced the family to seek shelter in Newport Workhouse. After brief employment with a local farmer Sophie obtained a position as chambermaid in the George Hotel, Portsmouth. From here she went to London and worked as a servant in a high-class brothel in Piccadilly where she became mistress of the exiled Duc de Bourbon, afterwards known as Prince of Condé. She was ambitious, and the Prince provided her with a good education not only in modern languages but in Greek and Latin.

''Ale of Wight' bitter from Goddards is a local favourtite.

He took her to Paris and, to prevent scandal and to qualify her to be received at court, had her married in 1818 to Adrien-Victor de Feuchères, a major in the royal guards. The Prince

Right: The incredible Sophie Dawes became far more famous than her drunken smuggling father.

supplied her dowry and promoted her husband to be his aide-de-camp and a baron.

Persuading the Duc to leave her a fortune in his will she was suspected of his murder when he was found dead, hanging from a window. Sophie died in 1840 but the St Helens' churchyard contains her

A dozen doors along from the Vine stands the wisteria-covered cottage where Sophie Dawes was born.

TO THE MEMORY,
OF JAMES DAWES
BARON DE FLASSANS,
WHO DIED SUDDENLY
AT CALAIS,
ON LANDING FROM ENGLAND
ON THE 23RD OF APRIL 1851
IN THE 45TH YEAR
OF HIS AGE,
LEAVING HIS WIDOW,
HIS FAMILY
AND FRIENDS TO WEEP
AND LAMENT THEIR LOSS.
"IN THE MIDST OF LIFE
WE ARE IN DEATH."

ERECTED AS A MARK OF
AFFECTION BY HIS AUNT
THE BARONESS DE TEUCHERS.

magnificent memorial to her nephew James Dawes who she was also suspected of poisoning because he knew too much.

Dawes was not the only name associated with smuggling at St Helens. During the period 1830 to 1851, when Customs prosecution details are available, the following characters were prosecuted for 'carrying & conveying' tubs of spirits: Cornelius Jones, Isaac Nicholas (who was caught on the Green), and James Weight (caught with a 3 gallon tub of French brandy near Brading Sluice). Unable to pay the £110 fine they were imprisoned at Winchester for six months.

Sophie Dawes, the smuggler's daughter who became known as 'The Queen of Chantilly'.

William Thomas Vine of Bembridge, James Attrill of Bembridge and J. Dyer of St Helens were caught and each sentenced to serve in the Navy for five years. Women also were involved. On 3 September 1836 James Brading, Samuel Warn, Harriet Bensey and Jane Wearne (alias Matilda Street) were apprehended. The first four were given six months imprisonment but Jane Wearne was sentenced to nine months because it was her second offence.

On 7 February 1838 Jacob Rogers and Thomas Tansom were sentenced to six months hard labour in the 'House of Correction at Winchester' for being 'assembled with others at the Parish of St Helens for the purpose of carrying and conveying 59 casks containing 182 gallons of brandy.'

Of particular interest are the cases of Richard Dawson, butcher and James (John) Midlane, mariner and innkeeper.

Opposite: The memorial in the village churchyard to Sophie Dawes' nephew James who she is believed to have poisoned because he knew too much.

The view across Bembridge Harbour to
St Helens' contraband landing beaches.

This dishonest couple were convicted on 21 January 1837 offering bribes to the Preventive Men in order to run some contraband goods. They were each fined £200 which they were unable to pay even when mitigated to £100, so were imprisoned and their boat, *The Lady Hope*, was sawn in half at Portsmouth Dockyard.

In one of the most unusual smuggling stories I have encountered, it is said John Midlane used to hide contraband in a pigsty he had created in his loft. Once hanging in the saloon bar of the Vine Inn was an oil painting entitled 'The Smuggling Gang' which included portraits of John and his eldest son Captain Charles Midlane.

A little over 100 years old the Vine Inn stands next to The Sailor's Home, the original stone-built 'smugglers' pub, now a private house. Refurbished in the last few years to create a light, airy space, the Vine has cosy raised drinking areas with a darts board and pool table at the rear.

Fresh home-cooked food is served seven days a week with steak and curry nights in the winter months. This community-focused pub has live music nights, a quiz night and even a bingo night. In addition to Doom Bar and Gales HSB Goddards 'Ale of Wight' is a regular feature.

Bembridge
Crab & Lobster

32 Forelands Field Road, Bembridge PO35 5TR

Tel: 01983 872244

www.crabandlobsterinn.co.uk

Bembridge is a beautiful location overlooking the eastern entrance to The Solent. Here it is possible to seek out the peaceful surroundings of Forelands, far from the main tourist areas. On old maps, this extreme north-easterly corner of the Island, is marked as 'Binbridge Isle,' bounded on one side by the sea at Brading Haven and on the other by the flooded marshland at Sandown.

During the eighteenth century Bembridge was a small village dependent on fishing, victualling ships at anchor off shore and smuggling. Expansion of Bembridge began after 1825 when Edward Wise inherited a considerable estate and

Perched on low cliffs within yards of the shore, and prettily adorned with flower baskets in summer, it's not surprising this tucked-away pub is such a popular destination.

people started building Regency villas around the area of the church.

CRAB & LOBSTER

The Crab & Lobster is renowned throughout the Island for daily deliveries of freshly caught seafood from fishermen working in view of the pub.

The Morton family was instrumental in bringing the railway to Bembridge, establishing a ferry conveying horses and carriages, and a passenger steamboat service to Portsmouth. The steam launch *Blanche* that plied between Bembridge and Portsmouth was run by 'Quilly' Smith and his brother.

The siblings were notorious smugglers, and used to meet their cronies in the Crab and Lobster Inn at Forelands. 'Quilly' would slip over to France in a fishing boat, returning with spirits and lace which were then hidden in Lane End Copse. A cave in Culver Cliff was also a hiding-place for smuggled goods.

Two hundred years ago mother-of-pearl (nacre) was a much favoured jewellery item. One seizure of the ornately coloured shell at Bembridge, taken off a ship returning from the Far East, was valued at £200 – about £12,000 today.

On 15 January 1831, nineteen-year-old Henry Dyer, of Bembridge was caught at St Helens 'carrying and conveying' a 3 gallon keg of Geneva Gin. At his trial the Customs Board requested he should be made to serve in the Navy but Magistrates, who considered he was not a seaman, fined him the statuary £100. Unable to pay he was committed to Winchester Gaol.

James Bay of Bembridge was arrested on board a smuggling vessel on 24 June 1832. His cargo of 20 tubs containing a total of 50 gallons of brandy was seized and a week later he was convicted and sentenced to serve in His Majesty's Navy.

On 2 February 1833 William Thomas Vine and James Attrill both of Bembridge and J. Dyer of St Helens were apprehended carrying and conveying spirits and each sentenced to serve in the Navy for five years. Dyer was found unfit, fined £100 and committed to Winchester Gaol for non-payment.

On 9 February 1833 Harriett Harbor of Bembridge was caught conveying and concealing ½ gall of brandy in two (animal) skins and one bladder. She was convicted and unable to pay the fine of £25, was imprisoned.

Two other women caught with Harriett were Mary Ann Fagan conveying and concealing seven skins containing 1 gallon of brandy and Mary Ann Fry (alias Maria) conveying and concealing six Skins containing 1 gallon of brandy.

There is little more summery than an alfresco meal at the Crab & Lobster but picnic sets on the terrace are in demand.

The interior is roomier than you might expect with lots of yachting memorabilia and old local photographs. **Below:** The adjacent cottage, which traded as the Holbrook's Tea Room until 1922, now houses the restaurant.

This extension to the main dining room has a very nautical feel.

Summons could not be served on these ladies by the Coast-guard because they were not from the Island, or not to be found. Consequently their cases could not be brought forward.

Mollie Downer was another leading spirit in the smugglers' gangs. Reputed to be a witch, she lived in Hill Way in a house called 'The Witch's Cottage' which had been in the Downer family since 1558. Mollie died in 1835, leaving the property to the Vicar, Sir Henry Thompson, who had it burned down.

Perched on low cliffs within yards of the shore, and prettily adorned with flower baskets in summer, this tucked away pub is such a popular destination, renowned throughout the Island for daily deliveries of freshly caught seafood from fishermen working in view of the pub.

There is little more summery than an alfresco meal at the Crab & Lobster but picnic sets on the terrace are in demand. Magnificent views of The Solent can also be enjoyed from the dining area and some of the bedrooms. The interior is roomier than one might expect with lots of yachting memorabilia and old local photographs, and a blazing fire in winter.

Expansion to Bembridge began after 1825 when Edward Wise inherited a considerable estate and people began to build Regency villas around the area of the church.

Little is known of the inn's early history but a nameless building appears on the 1862 map. This was probably the original inn where smugglers met to plan their next contraband run. Liquor licensing laws were introduced in 1870 and the Crab & Lobster became the focal point for Coastguards and fishermen.

The inn's continued prosperity is indicated by evidence of many alterations and extensions over the years. Most of the development occurred during the 1930s when visitors flocked to the Island. The adjacent cottage, which traded as Holbrook's Tea Room until 1922, was acquired by the brewers who leased it to various tenants before incorporating it into the present day inn. It now houses the restaurant.

Beers include Sharp's Doom Bar, Green King IPA and Fuggle-Dee-Dum, a chestnut, tawny red Premium Ale brewed by Goddards at their Barnsley Farm brewery in Ryde.

Taking centre stage among the real ales is Fuggle De Dum Premium Ale.

Rookley
The Chequers Inn

Chequers Inn, Niton Road, Rookley PO38 3NZ

Tel: 01983 840314

www.chequersinn-iow.co.uk

This country free house is regularly recommended by CAMRA and features repeatedly in the Good Beer Guide.

Close to the geographical centre of the Island, the small village of Rookley was for more than 150 years the epicentre of smuggling activities and claims the crown as Southern England's smuggling capital.

The village green, which was laid out to mark Queen Elizabeth's Silver Jubilee in 1977, has recently been enlarged and is an ideal place for sitting and studying the village display map or enjoying a picnic.

The Chequers is one of the most popular pubs on the Isle of Wight and has three luxury bed and breakfast rooms.

The old clay pits at Rookley belonged to the largest brick-works on the island. They have now been landscaped to become Rookley Country Park, consisting of a caravan park, lakes, children's amusements and a 'new' pub.

The Isle of Wight Foxhounds continue the traditional weekly meet at the Chequers from late summer to the end of March.

Until its expansion during the last century this former hamlet was focused on the junction of the roads from Godshill and Niton. It was the hub from where free traders' trails radiated, linking smuggling villages and towns from Brighstone in the west to Sandown in the east.

Rookley village was the first stop and storage dump for newly run contraband and all approaches to this smugglers' garrison were guarded day and night. It became a no-go area for all but the bravest Revenue Men. Smugglers who met at the Chequers had the opportunity of swapping intelligence about all aspects of the trade, including which Customs Officers could be bribed and which intimidated.

The goods were transported north from Rookley, some being sold along the way to customers at local inns and manor houses with the majority being exported across The Solent to the English mainland.

Expanded enormously from its original core, the pub has retained much of its traditional character.
Below: Hunting has always been a way of life hereabouts and is reflected in the pub's presentation.

George and Abraham Attrill from Rookley were among five men charged on 24 October 1836 with plundering the wreck of the *Clarendon* which came to grief two weeks earlier near Niton.

Although emphasis is on dining, the Chequers still retains a traditional pub bar at its heart.

Ironically, the earliest recollections of the building are of a 'Customs House' which at one time was called 'The Star'. By 1799, now renamed the Chequers, it had become the centre of the Island smuggling trade and was run by George Morris who paid 6d as a quarterly rate to the parish of Godshill.

Robert Downer ran the pub in 1820 paying 2s 4d as quarterly rates. In 1889 it became the property of the Mew Langton Royal Brewery Limited who leased it to James Reynolds (a distant relative of Sir Joshua Reynolds, first president of the Royal Academy of Art) for the monthly rental of 15 shillings.

In the early 1890s James's eldest daughter, Mary became licensee and she and her sister Bella remained in occupancy

for nearly sixty years. Many stories survive about these two extraordinary ladies who some people still remember.

During the 1960s and '70s the pub had something of a revival with several changes of landlord. But in 1986 Whitbread, who had swallowed up the Mew Langton empire, made the extraordinary decision to close the pub as an unviable commercial prospect. Permission to change the use to a private dwelling was refused and the property was purchased by a local farming couple, Sue and Richard Holmes.

There are extensive countryside views from the large garden which has great facilities for children including an outdoor adventure playground and a giant games area.

A short distance from the village, this country pub is one of the most popular on the Isle of Wight. It now includes three luxury bed and breakfast rooms, is regularly recommended by CAMRA and features repeatedly in the Good Beer Guide.

Expanded enormously from its original core the Chequers has retained much of its traditional character and is extremely popular for family groups with a children's menu and a carvery served every lunchtime. Beers include Forty Niner and Best Bitter from Hampshire's Ringwood Brewery and Jennings Lake District 'Cocker Hoop', a golden bitter from an all malt brew, with Styrian Golding hops added at various stages, to give a classic hop flavour and aroma.

Beers include Forty Niner and Best Bitter from Hampshire's Ringwood Brewery and Jennings Lake District 'Cocker Hoop'.

Shanklin
Chine Inn
1 Chine Hill, Shanklin PO37 6BW

Tel: 01983 865880

Shanklin Chine painted in 1791 by Samuel Howitt at the height of the smuggling era. The view shows the Chine Inn (top right) and the former Honeymoon Cottage in the centre built on a sandstone ridge.

Situated on the busy southeast coast of the Island, Shanklin lies halfway between the popular resorts of Sandown and Ventnor. Prior to 1864 it was a quiet village with a church, two hotels, an inn and several cottages but the arrival of the railway initiated the transformation from a small village to a bustling Victorian seaside watering place.

The original community was clustered around the head of the Chine and is known as Shanklin Old Village. Many of the buildings, still surviving today, contain clues to the village's smuggling past. Vernon Cottage is one of the most prominent places on the High Street. Now a very popular tea room

The Chine Inn painted by Thomas Rowlandson in 1791.

where the main lounge has a double floor which once served as storage for contraband. It is said a secret tunnel from the wine cellar led to the Chine Inn.

This interior titled 'Kitchen at Shanklin Chine' was painted by Rowlandson and the couple's intimate embrace suggests it was the Kingswell's 'Honeymoon Cottage'.

Tower Cottage nearby was built in 1825 on land leased from Shanklin Manor estate and, in 1937, road subsidence revealed a secret underground passageway leading to the Chine Inn. Smuggling became so prevalent that Revenue Officers from

an Excise Cutter were stationed at Jessamine Cottage, Rectory Road in the Old Village until the Watch House near the Chine was built in 1820.

In 1819 when John Keats stayed in Eglantine Cottage (now renamed Keats Cottage) and found inspiration from life on the Island and Shanklin Chine in particular, he wrote: 'The wondrous Chine here is a very great Lion; I wish I had as many guineas as there have been spy-glasses in it.'

Although treacherous on dark nights, especially before the pathways were created, Shanklin Chine was the ideal entry point for unloading and moving contraband. In 1817 William Colenutt excavated the present path through the Chine and opened it to the public. By 1873 visitors were expected to

Perched on top of Shanklin Chine since 1621 this gem of a stone-built pub lost its original thatched roof in a fire in 1859.

contribute 6d (2.5p) and amazingly the fee remained at this figure until 1958.

For some time the Chine remained a favourite smugglers' haunt. The path through the deep cut ravine was obscured from view by dense brushwood and small trees providing good cover for smugglers transporting contraband from the sandy beach up to the village.

One of the regular Chine Inn meetings of the clay pipe puffers club?

One Sunday afternoon 40 or 50 men were observed coming from the shore in procession, each carrying two kegs of

contraband spirits across his shoulders. Hurriedly they turned from the main highway into Sibden Road and disappeared.

Perhaps someone has just been playing 'Roll out the Barrel' on the old piano.

In the eighteenth century the Chine was a rough walk but the intrepid few who struggled as far as the waterfall were deeply impressed by its beauty and grandeur. Reference is made to early efforts to 'open the Chine up' to make it more accessible for mounted Excise Officers to lead their horses down to the beach.

The only residents at Shanklin Chine were the fisherman cum innkeeper and his family plus a labouring man and his wife, members of the Kingswell family, who had a reputation for smuggling. The Kingswells lived in Honeymoon Cottage just below the inn, so named because of the number of newly weds who stayed there.

Coastal erosion has truncated many of the Island's chines at the seaward end, and modern development has dissipated the essential character of others. However, the wooded slopes of Shanklin Chine retain much of their original atmosphere, despite the tarmac path and entrance fee.

Standing since 1621, this is one of the oldest licenced houses on the Island. Perched above the Chine on the pathway to the beach the pub enjoys stunning views out to sea over Shanklin Bay.

Beers on offer include Ventnor Gold and Timothy Taylor's Landlord drawn straight from the cask.

From 1839 William Prouten and his wife Frances (née Daish) ran the Chine Inn until the 1880s, when it became known as the Victoria Chine Inn. Like many rural innkeepers at the time William Prouten was also a farmer who grazed his cattle on

From the conservatory dining room windows there are stunning views down into the chine and out to sea over Shanklin Bay.

the meadows which are now part of Rylsone Gardens opposite Vernon Cottage.

A number of present day businesses, including the local coach
company still trade under the name of Daish. The prestigious
Daish's Hotel, standing in the old town High Street opposite
Vernon Cottage, was built by the family in 1833.

It seems that Frances Daish might have married beneath her
station when she wed William Prouten. At the time the Chine
Inn provided ale and broiled bacon to smugglers and there

The view down into
the Chine with the
Fisherman's
Cottage pub below.

are rumours of a tunnel that ran to the sea. On 21 February 1835 William and Josh Prouten were committed to Winchester Gaol for non-payment of a fine when they were caught smuggling 19 gallons of foreign spirits near Shanklin.

Bill Downer, the present owner, bought this quaint stone-built gem of a pub in 1992 and lovingly refurbished it, retain-

Bill Downer, the present landlord, who bought the pub in 1992.

ing much natural character and original charm. Bill found what he thought to be an internal well that had been filled with rubble. After some excavation he concluded it was most likely a former contraband store as it opened out into a large chamber towards the bottom. Refilling the chamber and shaft he sealed the opening with the cover still seen today in the dining room floor.

An interesting and varied menu in the dining area offers snacks, main courses and wonderful desserts. The main bar provides a range of beers including Ventnor Gold and Timothy Taylor's Landlord drawn straight from the cask.

The covered entrance to what was originally thought to be a well, opened out into a large chamber.

Situated right on the beach at the foot of Shanklin Chine, this unique thatched pub dates from 1817.

Shanklin
Fisherman's Cottage

3 Chine Hill, Shanklin PO37 6BW

Tel: 01983 866432

www.shanklinchine.co.uk

Shanklin shares the large bay on the southeast of the Island with Sandown but is quieter, with fine Victorian buildings and green open spaces. Its main feature is the Chine – a deep narrow ravine cut into the soft rock by water. Although it was a noted haunt of smugglers at the time, this natural beauty spot was developed in 1817 for the enjoyment of tourists.

The famous leafy gorge with its winding, woodland path, and steep sides was much loved by poets, artists and writers and remains a magical place with rare plants, wildlife and enchanting waterfalls.

The overwhelming theme of Shanklin's history is its covert smuggling activities. Throughout the eighteenth century and well into the nineteenth, many inhabitants were involved in illegal operations to bring in contraband, mostly from France, whilst avoiding the ever watchful eye of the Customs Men.

The famous smugglers' gorge with its winding woodland path, and steep sides became much loved by poets, artists and writers.

In June 1859 after many days 'creeping' offshore with grappling hooks to locate weighted sunken contraband, Coastguards were rewarded when they discovered 36 x 4½ gallon tubs and a flagon of spirits. In May 1862 some boys who were bird-nesting at Gills Cliff discovered 62 flagons. They tapped one and soon became oblivious of everything. By the time the Coastguards arrived, the contraband had disappeared but five flagons were found later in the outbuildings of Steephill Farm.

On another occasion, a number of men were seen busily engaged in digging out tubs from the sand between the ledges toward Luccombe. Shortly afterwards the Excise Man from Sandown, who had either observed or been informed of what was going on, was seen hastily leading his horse down the chine steps. Remounting at the bottom he rode rapidly toward the spot hoping to secure the prize, but before he got there the objects of his pursuit had been spirited away. The last known contraband run at Shanklin Chine was as late as 1881.

The present Luccombe village, a mile to the south, is a secretive place preceded centuries ago by a fishermen's hamlet on a ledge below, close to the sea. To reach the hamlet from land there was a 300 foot scramble down the cliff. At the bottom were eight cottages and, tradition states, two chapels. The inhabitants made a precarious living from the sea, virtually cut off from the landward side. When anyone died the body had to be rowed across the bay to Shanklin.

The Kingswells, the Buttons and the Kemps made up most of the community. One regular Sunday worshipper, 'Pound

The interior of the pub lives up to expectations with small low-beamed flagstoned rooms.

Old local pictures are displayed on the stripped stone walls.

Vectis Venom and Wight Gold Bitters are from the Island Brewery.

Hammer' Kingswell, fisherman and opportunist smuggler had his own seat in one of the chapels close to the door so he could continue to chew tobacco and spit outside without leaving the service.

There is a wonderful old photograph of Pound Hammer and his wife taken in the main room of their cottage at Luccombe. Of particular interest is the rear wall lined with samples from a wallpaper book acquired by them and put to good use!

It has been said that Mrs Kingswell thought nothing of walking to Wheeler's Bay near Ventnor to buy coal and carry it home on her back. Life must have been incredibly hard for the inhabitants of Luccombe village and not envied by anybody. This hardy lifestyle came to an abrupt end in 1910 when a mammoth landslide carried much of the ledge away.

Fisherman's Cottage was built in 1817 by the same William Colenutt who made the path through the Chine. He was also

In this Victorian illustration of Fisherman's Cottage with Honeymoon Cottage in the centre, the Chine Inn is just visible behind the trees at the top right.

From 1817 tourists paid 6d to visit the Chine.

In 1845 William Colenutt leased the cottage to his son-in-law, James Sampson who offered warm baths and sea bathing.

Pond Hammer Kingswell, fisherman and opportunist smuggler, with his wife in their cottage at Luccombe.

the first to operate bathing machines. In 1845 the cottage was leased to his son-in-law, James Sampson.

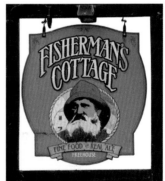

Members of the Colenutt family occupied the cottage until 1960 when, during a terrible storm, Miss Colenutt was rescued from her kitchen by Charlie Spencer of the Chine Inn. Charlie had heard Miss Colenutt ringing her bell for help after her kitchen was flooded by two feet of water. The Chine also suffered damage and required substantial and expensive repairs.

Nestling on the beach at the foot of Shanklin Chine, this unique thatched pub dates from 1817. The interior lives up to expectations with small low-beamed, flagstoned rooms and stripped stone walls displaying old local pictures. The Fisherman's Cottage restaurant is open daily between March and the end of October. Included on the menu is a variety of vegetarian dishes with a daily specials board, while Vectis Venom and Wight Gold Bitters are from the Island Brewery. From the sun soaked terrace there is a lovely seaside walk to Luccombe village and Chine.

Whitwell
White Horse Inn

High Street, Whitwell PO38 2PY

Tel: 01983 730375

www.whitehorseiow.co.uk

Built in 1454 this pub is one of the oldest not only in the Isle of Wight, but in the whole of the UK.

THE WHITE HORSE

Formerly the White Horse Ale House & reputed to be the oldest Inn on the Island dating from the 15th. Century, where a warm welcome with traditional George Gale Beers & Country Wines, and an exclusive selection of Home Cooked Fayre can be found.

The White Horse dispensed ale to fifteenth-century pilgrims who came to visit the White Well.

Whitwell is a small village on the south of the Island, 3 miles north west of Ventnor and a five minute drive from the neighbouring small villages of Godshill and Niton. It is thought that the village is named after the 'White Well', visited by large numbers of early pilgrims. There are medieval wall paintings in the church and the traditional custom of well dressing takes place in summer.

The old pub, much as the smugglers would have known it.

Northeast of Whitwell, on the estate of Wydcombe, is the shell of Appuldurcombe meaning 'valley of the apple trees', once the grandest house on the Isle of Wight. Standing in grounds designed by 'Capability' Brown the 1701 east front of this important example of English baroque architecture, has now been restored. The house is located west of the village of Wroxall, named after the wroc, a common name for buzzard.

Whitwell folk also played their part in smuggling activities. Ralph Stone, whose father and many other relations had been actively connected with contraband in their day, became locally known as 'The Great Smuggler'.

He always dressed as a gentleman farmer in loose velveteen shooting coat and waistcoat, a white hat, fancy trousers and wellington boots. His manner was so quiet, his conversation so easily disarming

Today the White Horse has a fine reputation for its food.

The stone-built original bar has been extended more than once to provide additional space for dining. **Below:** The ceiling of the family function room dining area is decorated with collection of old tools and farming implements.

and he had so much tact, energy and foresight that he became a commanding figure in local history, never suggesting the desperate risks he often ran.

He was a wonderful seaman but his vessel was seized nevertheless on occasions, and he served periods as a 'debtor to the Crown'. Unable or unwilling to pay fines, he was imprisoned in Winchester Gaol but despite this, he left a considerable fortune on his death, saved from the illicit trade he had carried on over many years.

The hand-chosen selection of real ales will bring a smile to any true devotee and includes Greene King IPA, Brakspear's 'Double Dropped' Bitter, Banks's Bitter and Wychwood's Hobgoblin.

In 1768, the seventeen-year-old Richard Worsley became the seventh Baronet, inheriting the wealthy 11,500 acre estate of Wydcombe and Appuldurcombe House. Seven years later he married the teenage heiress Seymour Dorothy Fleming, whose life was dramatised in the 2015 television film, *The Scandalous Lady W*. Sir Richard encouraged his wife to take lovers (rumoured to be as many as 27) so he could watch their lovemaking through the keyhole of the bedroom door.

He was a complicated, hypocritical man, happy to buy contraband from smugglers whilst believing that the place for the local destitute was in the workhouse which he was instrumental in founding at Newport in 1774, becoming one of the first trustees.

Originally known as 'The House of Industry' this grim place was the second in the country and the first on a large, almost industrial scale, capable of housing seven hundred inmates.

Today the pub has a tiled roof having suffered a fire in the thatched roof in 1987 and again twenty years later.

Outside is a large car park and a beer garden with picnic tables set among the trees.

Worsley's initiative became the model for workhouses nation-wide following the 1834 Poor Law Amendment Act. On his death, Wydcombe passed to his estranged wife Seymour and became separated from the core of the Appuldurcombe estate.

The shell of Appuldurcombe, once the grandest house on the Isle of Wight, stands in grounds designed by 'Capability' Brown.

As a girl, Sophie Dawes, daughter of smuggler Dickie Daws from St Helens, spent time with her destitute family in the Newport Workhouse (as we saw in the chapter on the Vine Inn, St Helens). From this lowest of low beginnings she went on to reach the very highest echelon of French society through being the mistress of the Prince de Condé, who many believe she later murdered.

Sophie had a niece Matilda (or someone whom she called her niece); some historians say she was Sophie's unacknowledged daughter. In an effort to find a suitable husband for Matilda Sophie connived with Charles Maurice de Talleyrand, a French bishop, politician and diplomat who worked at the

Far left: Charles Maurice de Talleyrand, conspiratorial ally of smuggler's daughter Sophie Dawes.

Left: Sophie Dawes, seen here at the height of her powers, who at the age of six spent time in the Newport House of Correction established by Sir Richard Worsley twenty-four years earlier.

highest levels of successive French governments. Those he served often distrusted Talleyrand but, like Napoleon, found him extremely useful. His very name has become a byword for crafty, cynical diplomacy. Talleyrand later was on very good terms with Sophie, and jointly they decided to make a match between his young nephew, the Marquis de Chabannes de La Palice and Miss Matilda Dawes.

Sophie's surviving family benefited from the accrued legacy of her scandalous life by acquiring prestigious property in the Island. Her nephew Edward Dawes was presented with Gotten Manor and William Henry Dawes, the estate of Wydcombe, while much of her money passed to her niece, Sophie Thavaron. William took possession of Wydcombe in about 1844 and

Seymour Dorothy Fleming, whose life was dramatised in the 2015 television film, *The Scandalous Lady W.*

Sir Richard Worsley became the seventh Baronet, inheriting the wealthy 11,500 acre estate of Wydcombe and Appuldurcombe House.

created the park thus completing a link in the astonishing rags to riches story of the smuggler's daughter.

Built in 1454 this pub is one of the oldest not only in the Isle of Wight, but in the whole of the UK and was obviously a favourite of fishermen, smugglers and other hard drinking men. In 1763 James Coleman, returning home to Wrongs Farm after drinking at the White Horse took a wrong route towards the cliff in the Undercliff. His horse stopped, but James fell from the saddle and over the edge, dying of his wounds a few days later.

Today the White Horse has a fine reputation for its food and the original stone-built bar has been extended more than once to provide additional dining space. All food is Island produce, home prepared and cooked. The menu includes signature grills and steaks and a quality selection of gluten-free and vegetarian options and the impressive list of specials changes every day.

The hand-chosen selection of real ales will bring a smile to any true devotee and includes Greene King IPA, Brakspear's 'Double Dropped' Bitter, Banks's Bitter and Wychwood's Hobgoblin.

Outside is a large car park and a beer garden with picnic tables set among the trees.

The White Lion stands at the cross roads in the centre of the smuggling village of Niton.

Niton
White Lion
High Street, Niton PO38 2AT

Tel: 01983 730293

Niton has most of the necessary components to make an ideal village: church, school, public library, several shops, attractive cottages and, of course, a pub. The village is in two parts, the more important being a little inland from Lower Niton (or Niton Undercliff).

The main village is 4½ miles due south of the central contraband clearing area of Rookley. Sydney Dobell's observation has previously been quoted: 'The whole population here are smugglers'. It is therefore not surprising to learn that tombs

The attractive whitewashed stone building has been a pub since at least 1744 when it was leased to John Clark.

Right: Among the changing selection of beers one can find Ringwood Fortyniner; Charles Wells Bombardier; Green King IPA and Adnams Lighthouse.

in the graveyard of St John the Baptist parish church, were regularly used for hiding contraband.

'Ye Old Cottage' opposite the church gates has bedroom windows peeping out from under the deep thatch. When word came that Coastguards were active in the area while smugglers were busy hiding tubs, a candle was placed in the very small window downstairs as a warning. One night smugglers climbed into a tomb to avoid detection and spent an uncomfortable night.

Thomas Morris, landlord of the White Lion had a good trade in smuggled goods. He boarded homeward bound ships off the coast and purchased tea, gloves, silk etc. On 17 September 1842 Morris was caught by Customs Men at Niton smuggling 3 gallons of Geneva gin. He couldn't pay the statutory £100 fine so was incarcerated in Winchester Gaol. In many such cases the felon was often the only bread winner so it was also terrible punishment for his family.

'Ye Old Cottage' opposite the church gate provided a warning system for smugglers hiding contraband in the churchyard.

The White Lion stands at the cross roads in the centre of Niton but no one quite remembers when the old stone built house became a pub. It was previously known as 'Speeds', and by 1744, when it was leased to John Clark, it was almost certainly a pub.

A candle was placed in the small window downstairs when word came that Revenue Men were active in the area.

Friendly and comfortable, The White Lion is the type of pub which has traditionally been the heart of British community life for hundreds of years. The interior has a cosy feel with a wood-burning stove in the brick fireplace of the popular public bar while the rest of the pub meanders away into games and dining areas.

There are food specials with something different nearly every day; 'pie day', 'curry evening' and great Sunday lunches. In addition to Ringwood Fortyniner, Charles Wells Bombadier, Green King IPA and Adnams Lighthouse they often have 'Undercliff Experience' on tap, an amber ale with a bitter sweet-malt-and-hops taste from Yates Isle of Wight brewery.

Tombs in the churchyard of St John the Baptist parish church, were used regularly for hiding contraband.

Located in the very heart of Niton, the village literally revolves around this pub, yet there is plenty of parking and a good size garden.

Niton
The Buddle Inn

St Catherine's Road, Niton PO38 2NE

Tel: 01983 730243

www.buddleinn.co.uk

The Island's most southerly pub, situated close to St Catherine's Light-house, was a favourite haunt of smugglers.

The road from Ventnor, running more or less parallel to the coast towards Blackgang, passes through some of the Island's most delightful scenery. The area, called in earlier times 'Under Wath', is now known as the Undercliff. Bounded on the landward side by high cliffs, the craggy rocks and wood-land on the seaward side offer fine views of the English Channel.

There can be few experiences more pleasurable than sitting in the sea-facing front terrace of the Buddle, enjoying a well prepared lunch and listening to the quiet strains of acoustic jazz and blues.

This historic pub is described as the Buddle 'Smugglers' Inn, and for good reason. During the smuggling era everyone hereabouts was in some way involved in the free trade. Sydney Dobell, Victorian poet and critic, visited this part of the Island for his health in 1860 and observed:

> 'The whole population here are smugglers. Everyone has an ostensible occupation, but nobody gets his money by it, or cares to work in it. Here are fishermen who never fish, but always have pockets full of money, and farmers whose farming consists in ploughing the deep by night, and whose daily time is spent standing like herons on lookout posts.'

Dobell also commented that the men of the village had a variety of pseudonyms, a characteristic shared by smugglers elsewhere in the country.

The Buddle Inn, situated in Niton Undercliff overlooking the famous lighthouse at St Catherine's Point, is the Island's most southerly pub. The unusual name of this old inn has been the subject of much speculation. One popular theory suggests it is derived from an old English word 'Bothele', meaning a dwelling.

The Buddle has an enviable reputation for good quality food using local produce and the freshest of freshly caught fish.

The building is thought to be at least 400 years old but is first mentioned when leased from the Lord of the Manor in 1776 and listed as 'Bundle Place'. A document of 1830 refers to it as 'Little Buddle or Bundle'. Sometime, during the next thirty years it had become a pub described in a will of 1859 as 'The Buddle Inn' and was known as a favourite haunt of smugglers.

There is an open fire in in the wide stone fireplace with its massive black mantle beam.

The traditional rooms in this attractive stone cottage pub retain plenty of character.

Notice the dimpled enigmatic smile on the young barman's face and the sign above his head 'HANDS OFF THE BARMAID'.

Below: Beyond the terrace and car park is a view of the smugglers' landing beach at Reeth Bay.

The well-defined smugglers' trail leading up from the Undercliff to the pub.

Known locally as the 'Pepperpot', this is all that remains of the early fourteenth-century St Catherine's Oratory on the downs above Blackgang. A resident priest would climb the curiously shaped tower and ensure a light was burning to guide shipping away from the dangerous coast.

The traditional rooms in this attractive stone cottage pub retain plenty of character. There is an open fire in the wide stone fireplace with its massive black mantle beam. The Buddle has an enviable reputation for good quality food using local produce and the freshest of freshly caught fish. Beers include the pub's own 'Buddle Brew' produced for them by Yates Brewery of Newchurch. On occasion they also have my own two favourite beers; Summer Lightning from Wiltshire and Timothy Taylor Landlord from Yorkshire.

To my mind there can be few experiences more pleasurable in life than sitting in the sea-facing front terrace of The Buddle and supping a pint of Summer Lightning while enjoying a well prepared lunch and listening to the quiet strains of acoustic jazz and blues.

The present lighthouse at St Catherine's Point was constructed in 1838 following the loss of the sailing ship *Clarendon* on rocks near the site.

Chale
The Wight Mouse Inn
Church Place, Chale PO38 2HA

Tel: 01983 730431

www.wightmouse.co.uk

The building on the right of the picture is the back of the present day pub. It was developed from the tap room and stables of the old wisteria-covered coaching inn.

Chale village lies at the foot of St Catherine's Down, a mile and a half from the Island's most southerly tip of St Catherine's Point. The parish stretches inland from the Military Road and the crumbling chalk and clay cliffs between Blackgang and Whale Chines, along a sheltered central vale to Chale Green in the north.

During the era of free trading this part of the Island's coast was particularly notorious for shipwrecks. James Wheeler, a member of Chale's most prominent smuggling family, kept a log from 1746 to 1808 recording details of 60 wrecks during the sixty-two year period. No effort was made to place a light

For a while the inn was known as the Clarendon but has reverted to its original name of the Wight Mouse.

The extensive dining area makes
the most of the stunning views
towards the cliffs of West Wight.

to warn ships of possible danger. Could this have been because impoverished villagers survived from plunder?

In the dim light of the morning of 11 October 1836, following a stormy night, early visitors to the cliff edge saw the *Clarendon*, a full rigged ship, battling against wind and sea endeavouring to beat off the dreaded lee shore.

Amongst those who followed the progress of the drama was John Wheeler. This tall, weather-beaten fisherman had previously served on a man-o-war. From the high cliffs he watched as the stricken vessel was swept around to the clearer area at Blackgang.

Although completely refurbished, the large fireplace stands in the area of the pub, formerly the tap room, used by the smugglers.

Newer timbers complement the older original beams.

Recognising there was now a dim hope some assistance might be given he dashed down the path at Cliff's End reaching the shore just before the crash came. Grabbing a coil of rope from a fisherman's hut he tied one end round his waist and threw the remainder to a mate. Then, racing down to the beach, he plunged into the surf where the vessel had struck and was being pounded by the seas.

Despite his courageous efforts, Wheeler managed to save only three men who one after the other had jumped over the side. In an amazing coincidence he recognised one of the men as a former shipmate he had rescued four years previously. Amongst those drowned was a Miss Gourlay and remarkably her body was carried by the tide and cast ashore opposite her father's house at Southsea. The ship was smashed to pieces and the remainder of the 25 passengers and crew were drowned or killed by broken debris crashing about in the surf.

The pub is now enormously popular with families drawn by its lovely location, large safe beer garden and good parking.

Many of the timbers from the destroyed vessel were later used in the construction of local houses and in extending the Wight Mouse. As a tribute the inn was renamed the Clarendon but has now reverted to its original name.

An artist's impression of the dramatic moment in 1836 when the *Clarendon* came to grief in Chale Bay claiming 25 lives.

Most of the crew and passengers from the doomed *Clarendon* are buried in St Andrew's church-yard near the Wight Mouse.

Members of the Wheeler Family photographed fifty years after the *Clarendon* disaster.

Box Cottage, Southdown Lane, now extensively refurbished, was the former home of the Wheeler smuggling family.

After the sinking of the Clarendon and much public pressure, a lighthouse was built on St Catherine's Down. Unfortunately the officials from mainland England had not accounted for the fogs which roll in from the sea obscuring the top of the downs and after further shipwrecks a second lighthouse, which is still in use, was built at the foot of the cliffs.

The present parish church of St Andrew, which dates from the fourteenth century, stands near the Wight Mouse. Some of the graves of the crew and passengers from the doomed *Clarendon* can be seen in the churchyard where there is a panoramic view of Chale Bay.

On 24 October 1836 the following were all convicted of plundering the wreck of the *Clarendon*: George and Abraham Attrill of Rookley (£20 or six months hard labour), William Haynes of Whitwell (£5 or two months imprisonment), William Gatrell of Brixton (one months imprisonment) and James Long of Chale (fined 15 shillings).

The Wheeler family, who were fishermen, smugglers, plunderers and occasional heroes lived in Box Cottage in Southdown Lane. Blackgang Chine was their main landing beach where a gigantic cave provided storage for their contraband. This whole area has subsequently disappeared in coastal erosion and landslips.

In Victorian England, affluent town dwellers were seeking new healthy holiday resorts, ideally near the coast. Destina-

The Back of Wight near Atherfield Point.

Blackgang Chine cave, now swept away by landslips and erosion, was used as a store for contraband and goods plundered from shipwrecks.

tions such as Torquay and Lyme Regis grew to be very popular. As the railway network spread further south, the Isle of Wight became an increasingly attractive holiday proposition and the Clarendon Hotel a desirable place to stay.

In 1843 Alexander Dabell established what has now become Britain's oldest theme park at Blackgang Chine. The most famous attraction of this general-purpose scenic, curiosity park was a large whale skeleton washed up near the Needles in 1842, and is still a showpiece today.

Blackgang Chine amusement park opened in 1843 was Britain's first theme park.

The Wight Mouse is now owned by Dorset brewers Hall & Woodhouse and continues to be enormously popular with visitors. Families are drawn here by its lovely location, large, safe beer garden and spacious parking. The newly refurbished dining area makes the most of the stunning views towards the cliffs in West Wight.

For imagination and value for money the extensive menu is amongst the most impressive anywhere. In addition to H&Ws Tanglefoot and First Call, there are at least three guest ales.

Shorwell
The Crown Inn
Walkers Lane, Shorwell PO30 3JZ

Tel: 01983 740293

www.crowninnshorwell.co.uk

This pretty, quiet little hideaway village lies south of Rowborough and Cheverton Downs.

Smugglers of Shorwell, supping ale in the Crown and sucking on their clay pipes must have considered themselves fortunate. Manor houses were traditionally amongst the smugglers' best customers and Shorwell has three: the Elizabethan North Court, the Jacobean Wolverton Manor and the Tudor West Court on Limerstone Road.

The three-hundred year old Crown is situated in the centre of this pretty, quiet little hideaway village.

Beers include Sharp's Doom Bar, Adnams Broadside and Fuggle, a chestnut, tawny red Premium Ale from Goddards Island Brewery. **Below:** The cosy cottagey feel is enhanced by a couple of winter log fires, one with a fancy tiled surround.

The village is a couple of miles inland from Brighstone Bay and a little over 3 miles west of Rookley, the main contraband clearing centre. Well-trodden smugglers' routes from Brighstone Bay led inland through Thorncross or Sutton before passing Wolverton Manor and arriving at the Crown.

The inn in parts dates from the early 1700s and varying floor levels bear witness to many alterations. The interior comprises four pleasant spacious rooms with good antique furniture around a central bar. An authentic country atmosphere pervades throughout with a mixture of carpet, tiles and flagstone floors. Old country prints decorate the stone walls of the beamed lounge and blue and white china is displayed on an attractive carved dresser. The cosy cottagey feel is enhanced by a couple of winter log fires, one with a fancy tiled surround. In the main dining room black wooden pews form bays around tables.

Old country prints decorate the stone walls of the beamed lounge and blue and white china is displayed on an attractive carved dresser.

In summer the tree-sheltered garden is very appealing.

In summer the tree-sheltered garden is very appealing with its ducks and a little stream broadening out into a trout filled pool. On the lawn are plenty of picnic-sets with additional white garden tables and chairs.

The Crown has a reputation for good value quality food from snacks and light bites to a full menu of pub classics, making the most of local produce and seafood. Beers include Sharp's Doom Bar, Adnams Broadside and Fuggle, a chestnut, tawny red Premium Ale from Goddards own Island Brewery.

As well as the annual garden fair, concerts are held throughout the year at Wolverton Manor.

The Three Bishops is essentially an old village pub with a large modern country restaurant extension.

Brighstone
The Three Bishops

Main Road, Brighstone PO30 4AH

Tel: 01983 740226

www.threebishopspub.co.uk

In 1973 the New Inn was renamed the 'Three Bishops' after three local celebrated clergymen.

With new residential development south of the historic centre, Brighstone is the largest village in Back of Wight. This friendly place enjoys a favourable position midway along the 12-mile stretch of the Island's south-west coastline. Adjacent to the 800-year-old Norman church is a rectory dating back to 1347, and a grave-yard where generations of smugglers have been laid to rest.

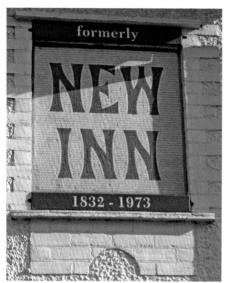

The original pub dates from the 1830s.

'Free trading' was a major occupation in Brighstone during the eighteenth and nineteenth centuries when fishing was a precarious occupation and farm workers' wages were 10 shillings (50 pence) per week. Smugglers rowed over to France and the Channel Islands in longboats to collect luxury goods which were secreted in a series of cleverly constructed hiding places in some of the local cottages.

One such cottage, built in 1704, seemed to author Richard Hutchins, designed for the express purpose of concealing contraband: 'Basically, there are four rooms, two up and two down; the ground floor rooms, connected by a short corridor, are divided by a vast chimney piece – formerly an inglenook and

The pub's oldest part is the elevated front bar.

The newer extension has a rustic feel featuring a great deal of wood and even a timber ceiling.
Below: Beers on offer include Doom Bar, Abbot Ale, Adnams Ghost Ship and Youngs Bitter.

baker's oven, which opens out on to the corridor. However, behind the oven is an enormous black cavity which extends upwards to the landing on the top floor. The only way into this cavity is from above, through a hole which at all times is sealed off and well-disguised by a heavy stone slab'.

In this photograph the new Inn advertises its tea garden. Beyond is the Five Bells (now a hairdressers) and the thatched village shop.

Some of the buildings still retain the image of a small square-rig sailing ship carved into the stone or chalk walls, believed to be a symbol indicating the occupants were sympathetic to smugglers. One such etched design can be seen on the flank wall of a cottage standing opposite the junction with North Street. In recent years a barrel of brandy was found down the road from Carrier Stable when a building was being converted.

Through most of the nineteenth century, the formerly small community had two public houses; the Five Bells and the New Inn, standing on opposite corners of Warnes Lane in the village centre. The Five Bells ceased trading as a pub after the First World War and is now the village hairdressers.

Some aspects of the present scene remain unchanged since the days of free traders.

Left: The original façade of the New Inn can be seen just beyond the Five Bells with St Mary's church on the far left.

In 1973 the New Inn was renamed the 'Three Bishops' after three local clergy, Samuel Wilberforce, Thomas Ken and George Moberly who were uniquely all appointed bishops. Samuel Wilberforce, son of William Wilberforce MP, became Bishop of Oxford and Thomas Ken who wrote the fine hymn, 'Awake my soul and with the sun' went on to become Bishop of Bath and Wells. After a distinguished academic career,

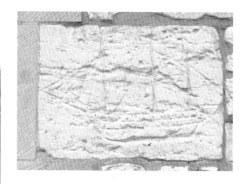

This smugglers' 'safe house' stands opposite the junction with North Street. **Right:** The small square-rig sailing ship design is believed by some to have been a networking symbol for the smugglers.

George Moberly retired to the Rectory of St Mary's church, Brighstone but in 1869 Prime Minister Gladstone elevated him to be Bishop of Salisbury.

Today the Three Bishops is essentially an old village pub with a large modern country restaurant extension at the rear and like other fine pubs is a family run business. The enthusiastic father and son team offer an extensive menu of pub classics using fresh local meat and fish.

In addition to the seemingly ubiquitous Sharp's Doom Bar, the beers on offer include Abbot Ale, Adnams Ghost Ship and Youngs Bitter. There is a large sunny garden, generous parking space and food is served from noon to 9:00 pm.

North Street in the centre of the village boasts some fine examples of thatched and stone buildings including the local library and museum.

The Sun Inn is a picture book thatched country pub in a charming peaceful setting.

Hulverstone
The Sun Inn

The Sun Inn, Hulverstone PO30 4EH

Tel: 01983 741 124

www.sun-hulverstone.com

In the southwest of the Island, less than a mile from the Undercliff shore, are three closely grouped hamlets; Hulverstone, Mottistone and Brook. Each has a cluster of stone built cottages whose earlier occupants were mainly fishermen smugglers and their families.

Hulverstone has a small, stone-built manor house, an old school building – now a residence – a former toll-house, and

Please mind the Step..

SUN
INN

The low-ceilinged bar with its feature fireplace
has old floorboards and flagstones with a nice
mix of traditional furniture. Furniture legs are
wedged with beer mats to stop tables wobbling
on ancient uneven flagstones where generations
of sea-booted smugglers have walked.

The old bar leads through to the sunny dining area with large garden-view windows. The pleasing mixture of floor levels is due to the slightly sloping ground on which the pub is built with the newer rooms added at a lower level.

Beers include the Sun Inn's own bitter, brewed for them by Goddards, along with a selection of regularly changing West-country ales.

the 400-year-old Sun Inn. Mottistone, enclosing a small unspoilt green has one of the most attractive manor houses on the Island. Brook is a one street village stretching from the foot of the downs in the north to the Military Road and the coast in the south.

Smuggling throughout the area simply became a way of life. Reverend Collingwood Fenwick, the landowning rector of Brook from 1833 to 1856 commented: 'The people engaged in smuggling or benefitting by it, do not feel it a moral offence and make no secret of their success when the danger is over'.

Contraband landed at Chilton Chine was transported inland by the notorious Mottistone Gang to Hulverstone before making the onward journey to Shalfleet and the north shore. One of the main routes for goods landed at Brook Bay was through the village, then due north to Shalcombe Cottages, just west of Churchills Farm, emerging at Wellow. The tubs were often hidden in Hundred Acres and in Wellow Brook before being moved on to the north coast when the way was clear.

At Mottistone a large tomb, excavated for the bodies of seven sailors washed ashore from a wreck, was used for storing contraband. The tower of the church was used as a seamark and lookout point, and the local gang used caves in the cliffs

Stunning scenery, with outstanding sea views, makes alfresco dining a delight, especially in summer months when flower borders are alive with colour.

Back of Wight provided ideal beaches for landing contraband.

The smugglers' route climbed the undercliff from Brook Bay.

above the beach for storage. Cottages at Mottistone nearest the sea had small windows cut high in the walls where a lookout could be stationed and warning lights placed. The manor at Mottistone was also pressed into service: tubs were stored in the large loft. It is reported that Revenue Men often looked in at the clap door, but did not dare venture up the rotten ladder.

Smugglers became adept at avoiding apprehension although some were caught and spent time in Winchester Gaol before the Island had any prisons of its own. Violence in avoiding arrest and securing smuggled goods was not unknown. On 9 January 1837 William Collier, a volunteer Coastguard, was pushed off the cliffs to his death by noted smuggler, John Moorman.

In 1831 Charles Seely married Mary Hilton and bought Brook House – now divided into apartments. The couple enlarged the property and quickly became part of Island life and society.

On 27 August 1842, members of the Mottistone gang William Cook, Andrew Cook, Reuben Cooper and Israel Chambers were caught 'Unshipping &c. seventeen Casks containing fifty two gallons of Foreign Brandy'. Three of them were acquitted but William Cook was convicted, and unable to pay the £100 fine, was sent to prison.

In 1958, Joe Morris of 2, Old Myrtle Cottage, Brook discovered a 6-gallon brandy cask and three glass bottles or jars of 4, 5 and 6 gallons capacity behind a bend in the chimney. Exactly the same type of 'hidey' was found in Wellow Cottage, once owned by authoress Mrs Campbell Barnes. During renovations a cavity beside the fireplace was discovered which opened to the loft above where tubs were once stowed.

Joe Morris outside 2, Old Myrtle Cottage, Brook in 1958 when smugglers' jars and a cask were found hidden in a bend in the chimney

Brook Hill House, with its commanding
position on the downs, was completed
in 1915 for Sir Charles Seely.

Described as an ale house owned by William Cooke, the Sun Inn was first mentioned in 1816 when it was sold to Benjamin Mew, a brewer of Crocker Street, Newport. It was already an established meeting place for smugglers. The 1841 and 1851 censuses cite an elderly man, John Moorman, as the innkeeper. By 1852 the inn was run by James Jacobs and by 1855 by Charles Wolfe, who was also a leather collar and harness maker.

Brook Cottage at Wellow on one of the main smuggling routes had a number of hiding places for concealed contraband.

In 1856, Charles Seely, a Nottinghamshire coal mine owner who had originally come to the Island as a boy to recover from TB purchased the Brook Estate including most of the village. In 1860 W. B. Mew sold the Sun Inn to Seely who promptly leased it back to the brewers. According to David Seely, Lord Mottistone, his great grandfather Charles

approved of the pub being in Hulverstone as: 'It meant the men would be sobered up by the time they got home, having walked in the fresh air back to Brook or Mottistone.' At that time the Sun was run by Henry W. Mussell and it is said that the walk home was also an opportunity for a good singsong.

The Sun Inn is a picture-book thatched country pub in a charming, peaceful setting with views over the Channel. The low-ceilinged bar with its feature fireplace has old floorboards and flagstones with a pleasant mix of traditional furniture. The feature brick and stone walls are decorated with horse brasses and ironwork.

Windows in the dining area overlook a large split level garden. The stunning scenery, with outstanding sea views makes alfresco dining a delight, especially in summer months when flower borders are alive with colour.

The extensive menu offers classic home-cooked dishes making the most of local meat, fish and vegetables. Beers include the Sun Inn's own bitter brewed for them by Goddards along with a selection of other regularly alternating Westcountry ales.

Situated in the quiet village street, The Red Lion has the feeling of a genuine local

Freshwater
The Red Lion
Church Place, Freshwater PO40 9BP

Tel: 01983 754925

www.redlion-freshwater.co.uk

The largest village in West Wight, Freshwater was named from the spring rising about 200 yards from the beach at Freshwater Bay and flowing north into the widening River Yar.

South of the village lies the small, picturesque, steeply shelving beach at Freshwater Bay covered in a mixture of grey flint and chalk pebbles producing a unique sound as the waves rise and fall onto the shore. Such a peaceful scene today makes it hard to believe a Preventive Officer was stoned to death here when he disturbed smugglers unloading contraband brandy from a boat.

When the chance of detection was slight, most free traders preferred to land goods on the southwest coast of the Island where there are several more accessible landing places than on the southeast, and all were regularly used. Along with the chines, favourite landing beaches here were at Freshwater Bay, Watcombe Bay and Scratchell's Bay.

Smugglers utilised caves scattered below the chalk cliffs which are exposed at low tide when explorers run the risk of being cut off by the incoming tide. It is best to check the tide tables for an abnormally low tide before venturing across the rocky exposed ledge to access the caves on the western side.

In 1836, Lieutenant Dornford and his crew of seven Coastguards, were charged with colluding with smugglers. Part of the evidence being their friendship with Mr Rogers of Compton Farm, 'a person', according to the Supervisor of Excise, 'in the habit of affording every accommodation to smugglers.'

The present substantial red-brick pub stands on the foundations of a much older inn dating from the eleventh century.

Goddards IOW and best bitters from Ruddles and Harveys of Sussex are often included among the changing beer selection.

The simple rustic interior has country-style furniture on flagstones and bare board floors.

The last recorded case of brandy smuggling involved kegs landed at Freshwater in 1870. Free trader Noel Wilkins was thought to be one of a gang of five smugglers landing tubs here, having moved his activities from the mainland for easier landings on the Island. Wilkins, who had been suspected for some time was eventually caught with tubs on

Ventnor beach. The brandy seized was found to be 60% over proof. He spent six months in jail but his four comrades escaped.

Comfort for mature locals is assured by the landlord's discouragement of young children in the bar and his reputation of fining mobile phone users £1 for any calls (proceeds to charity).

Situated in the quiet village street, the Red Lion has the feeling of a genuine local. It is close to the Causeway and Freshwater Way footpath connecting Yarmouth with the southern coast at Freshwater Bay. Standing next to the pub is the medieval All Saints church; one of the oldest on the Isle of Wight, and listed in the Domesday survey of 1086. Inside is a marble memorial commemorating Alfred Lord Tennyson. Several of his family members are buried in the churchyard.

Outdoor seating is provided in the quiet, carefully tended garden.

The present substantial red brick pub stands on the foundations of a much older inn dating from the eleventh century. The open-plan bar has a bustling atmosphere with open fires, low grey sofas and sturdy country style furnishings. Throughout are flagstones and bare-board floors and at one end of the bar a multitude of local pictures and photographs decorate the walls.

The Red Lion is situated close to the Causeway on the Freshwater Way footpath connecting Yarmouth with the southern coast at Freshwater Bay.

The menu in this simple rustic style pub boasts a varied cuisine showcasing local produce and home grown herbs. Outdoor seating is provided in the carefully tended garden. Picnic-sets in the quiet square in front of the pub provide a perfect place to relax with a cool drink on hot sunny days.

Freshwater smugglers utilised caves below the chalk cliffs which are exposed at low tide.

A Victorian extension to the pub resulted in this curious chimney arrangement forming the present day front elevation.

Totland Bay
Highdown Inn

Highdown Lane, Totland PO39 0HY

Tel: 01983 752450

www.highdowninn.com

A key to appreciating the Isle of Wight is to climb as high as possible and savour its spectacular vistas. One of the most impressive views can be seen by climbing Tennyson Down from Freshwater Bay up to the Tennyson Monument. From here one can see much of the Island and further to southern Hampshire. Visible on a clear day are Swanage and Old Harry Rocks, continuations of the same chalk ridge.

Becoming Poet Laureate in 1850 and the success of his poems *In Memoriam* and *Maud* enabled Alfred Lord Tennyson to buy Farringford House near to Highdown Inn at Totland. Many of his famous works including *Charge of the Light Brigade* and *Enoch Arden* were written during the forty years he lived here.

This early (pre-extension) photograph shows the road up to Highdown passing the pub's original front.

Five years after Tennyson's death a cross of Cornish granite was erected on High Down. The inscription reads: 'In Memory of Alfred Lord Tennyson this cross is raised. A Beacon to Sailors, by the People of Freshwater and other Friends in England and America'. The monument was unveiled in 1897 and is now maintained by Trinity House as a seamark.

The rocky coastline around Totland Bay for the most part is covered in a thick blanket of trees and greenery. The bay itself has a sandy beach, ideal for swimming, with clear turq-

The Highdown is a dog friendly place with a very relaxed atmosphere.

A chalk board above the bar attests to the Highdown's reputation for home cooked seafood dishes.

uoise waters and far reaching views to the mainland.

Highdown Inn, at the foot of Tennyson Down was a notorious smugglers' haunt. It is said that on one occasion Preventive Officers who called in looking for evidence of contraband were never seen to leave and no one ever heard of them again. It is alleged that after being knocked unconscious they were taken to the top of the down and their bodies were thrown on to the rocks some hundreds of feet below.

Beers include the pub's own 'Highdown Ale' brewed for them by Yates Isle of Wight brewery and the refreshingly light 'Fiddler's Elbow' from Wychwood.

Local smugglers used a large cave halfway down the chalk cliff at Main Beach Alum Bay. The huge storage cavern was completely unapproachable from top or bottom except by ropes and rope ladders. It was a perfectly secure hiding place for contraband which, when required for local customers or

Numerous picnic tables are set on a slightly raised area in the large beer garden.

forward distribution, was hauled up over the cliff top.

Towards the end of the smuggling era, the three Conway brothers, William, Charles and George, played a helpful part in the construction of the Needles Lighthouse. As young men the Conways had lived at Middleton Cottage, a stone's throw from Farringford and shipped contraband from France in their lugger appropriately named *The Brothers*. Tennyson's eldest son Hallam bought Middleton Cottage from the Conways when they moved to Colwell.

Lord Tennyson must have been fully aware of the local smuggling during his residency in the area. In the memoir of his father, Hallam says he was friendly with the longshoremen at Freshwater Bay and on occasion was rowed out by them into the bay where he would recite his poems. He found them a most receptive audience and no doubt these experiences

Farringford House, the former home of Poet Laureate Alfred Lord Tennyson.

helped him maintain the common touch in his work.

Highdown Inn, set at the foot of NT Tennyson Down, is a perfect example of a traditional country pub beloved by walkers, strollers and cyclists alike. The former public bar now serves as a smart little dining room and there is a larger restaurant. Numerous picnic tables are set on a slightly raised area in the large beer garden.

Considering its maritime location, the Highdown Inn is inevitably noted for its seafood and shellfish dishes and the seasonal menu also includes various home cooked meat and 'game' specialities served in generous portions with vegetables sourced locally.

Middleton Cottage, a stone's throw from Farringford, was home to the smuggling Conway brothers.

The smuggling Conway brothers, William, Charles and George sold Middleton Cottage to Hallam Tennyson when they moved to Colwell.

Tennyson took a daily walk on the down where there is now a sea-marker monument to his memory. **Inset:** From Tennyson Down, on a fine day, much of the Island is visible with views extending to southern Hampshire and even to Dorset.

It is alleged that two Preventive Officers, knocked unconscious in the pub, were carried to the top of the down and thrown to their deaths from the cliff tops.